NATURE-INSPIRED

POLITICAL COALITION AGREEMENT:

A BIOMIMICRY BLUEPRINT
FOR COLLABORATIVE GOVERNANCE

GAMELIHLE SIBANDA

Disclaimer

This book is not intended as an academic exercise. It does not engage in comparing previous research or publications with the proposals herein. Written in the form of a story, it represents a departure from conventional academic texts. This book is not a textbook, a manual, nor a piece of academic research. Instead, it embraces the art of storytelling, offering a unique narrative approach to its political themes. However, the biomimicry examples are founded on scientific knowledge.

Final Note

This book is designed to inspire those who are willing to take action, either by embracing the proposals presented or by offering alternative views. It is a call to action for proactive engagement and thoughtful discourse, encouraging readers to not only contemplate the ideas within but to actively participate in shaping their political landscape.

FOREWORD

Nature's wisdom transcends time and space, teaching us lessons of resilience, collaboration, and harmony. When we examine the intricate ecosystems around us, we find unparalleled examples of how diverse entities can coexist and thrive. In the realm of politics, as many nations navigate the complexities of coalition governance, nature can offer invaluable insights. This book aims to draw from the world of biomimicry (innovation inspired by nature) to provide a blueprint for a collaborative political future, ensuring a prosperity through unity of purpose.

INTENDED READER

This book is primarily aimed at individuals deeply engaged with the world of politics, including seasoned politicians, aspiring political figures, and those keen to understand the workings of coalition governments. It also aims to inspire the electorate – the voters who entrust politicians to make policy and political decisions on their behalf.

Upon reading this book, readers are likely to find themselves in one of three categories:

1. **The Improvers**: These readers largely agree with the proposals in the book and are motivated to offer additional improvements. They see the book's ideas as a foundation for further development and enhancement.

2. **The Alternatives Offerers**: This group disagrees with the proposals but in a constructive manner. They provide viable alternative solutions, enriching the political discourse with new perspectives and ideas.

3. **The Despondent**: The final group comprises those who disagree with the proposals and are engulfed in despair, believing the problems discussed are insurmountable. These readers view the book's suggestions as unfeasible, reflecting a sense of skepticism and disillusionment with the current political climate.

PROLOGUE:
REIMAGINING THE
NATURE OF COALITIONS

In the quietude of the African savannah, as the sun casts its golden hue, a lion – the apex predator – meanders through the grasslands. Yet, its reign is not unchallenged. Hyenas and other creatures pose threats to its cubs. This dynamic, an intricate dance of power and vulnerability, mirrors the complexities of political coalitions.

Traditionally, coalition politics has been viewed through a rather myopic lens. A majority takes the helm, governing, while the minority sits back, critiques, and, when discontented, threatens with votes of no confidence. It is akin to having a symphony where only half the orchestra plays while the rest wait for a single wrong note to pounce upon. Such an approach is inefficient and fails to harness the collective wisdom and expertise that each representative brings to governance.

Imagine a scenario where the entirety of the elected cohort of leaders, all 100%, is actively engaged in governance. Rather than lurking in the shadows, pointing out errors, every representative contributes their expertise, wisdom, and ideas. The collective energy, previously wasted in internal politics, is now channelled towards building a prosperous nation.

A common rebuttal to this proposition is the question of accountability. If everyone is on the inside, who holds the coalition accountable? My reflection leads me to a simple yet profound answer: the electorate. By establishing robust monitoring, evaluation, and transparency mechanisms, we can shift the oversight from internal politics to the public. The very people who elected the coalition should be its auditors. This not only ensures transparency but also nurtures a direct bond between the electorate and their representatives.

Of course, the fear of collective malfeasance or self-interests overshadowing progress looms large. But with the right structures, transparency measures, and genuine commitment to service, the coalition can function as a cohesive unit. The power to recall should be vested in the voters, not in opposing politicians driven by ambition and power dynamics. A coalition should stand or fall as a collective unit, not fragmented by individual or party interests. Imagine a race to the summit of the mountain. If the rules are that the first person to reach the summit will win the grand prize, each competitor will aim to outperform everyone else and probably not even stop to assist someone who collapses on the way. However, if the rules are changed so the prize is given to the group if all members reach the summit within an agreed time, teamwork becomes imperative.

Another intriguing dimension is decision-making. Drawing parallels from nature, while the lion might be the apex predator, it does not dictate the terms for every species in the ecosystem. Similarly, majority rule in coalitions should not overshadow the voices of smaller parties. Their perspectives, although representing a smaller constituency, might be the very insights needed to steer the nation in the right direction.

Majority influence can be subtle, allowing a larger party to shape narratives without overpowering smaller voices. Consensus and collaboration should be the foundation stones of decision-making, rather than sheer numerical strength. The melody of the smaller parties, though soft, carries a unique tune that can harmonize the entire symphony.

However, it is important to address some concerns raised by skeptics. Some argue that politicians pursue self-interests and will resist any change that challenges the status quo. While this may be true in certain cases, it does not mean that collaboration is impossible. The intention of this book is not to render politicians powerless or irrelevant. On the contrary, it aims to foster collaboration among politicians and between politicians and the electorate with one goal in mind – optimizing developmental outcomes for all citizens.

Some may argue that implementing these proposals could take centuries due to existing legislative frameworks. To address concerns about practical implementation, it is crucial to emphasize that transformative changes in the political system do not need to happen overnight or over centuries. Implementing proposals from this book requires a strategic approach focused on incremental changes and multidisciplinary collaboration. By forming change management committees comprising experts from various fields, revising laws and policies in alignment with biomimicry principles becomes attainable.

In this prologue, we have set the stage for what lies ahead – a journey into nature-inspired political coalition agreements where collective wisdom prevails over divisive politics and where harmony thrives amidst diversity. In each chapter that follows, we will explore different facets of this blueprint for collaborative governance, delving into methodologies, examples from nature, and practical strategies for implementation. Together, let us embark on a path towards a prosperous nation.

EXECUTIVE SUMMARY

In the dynamic political landscapes, where coalition governance is becoming increasingly prominent, there is a pressing need for strategies that ensure stability, inclusivity, and progress. This book delves deep into the principles of biomimicry, drawing inspiration from nature's intricate ecosystems, to provide a comprehensive blueprint for collaborative governance.

Key Insights:

1. **Nature as a Model:** Ecosystems, especially those with multiple keystone species, offer invaluable lessons in collaboration, balance, and resilience. The interplay between different species ensures the health and vitality of the entire system.

2. **Equitable Distribution:** Just as resources in nature are allocated to sustain diverse life, power and responsibilities in a coalition should be distributed equitably, based on representation.

3. **Balanced Predation:** Nature's balance between predators and prey underscores the importance of checks and balances in coalition governance, preventing dominance by any single party.

4. **Collaborative Habitat Creation:** Mutualistic relationships in nature emphasize the value of inter-party collaborations on national projects, ensuring diverse perspectives and holistic outcomes.

5. **Symbiotic Relationships:** The mutual benefits seen in nature's symbiotic relationships can be mirrored in policy partnerships and

shared platforms, where parties combine their expertise for the nation's benefit.

6. **Transparency and Accountability:** Drawing parallels with nature's clear waters and regulating forces, the book emphasizes the importance of transparency mechanisms and accountability frameworks in coalition governance.

7. **Harnessing the Ripple Effect:** Recognizing the interconnectedness inherent in political decisions, the book underscores the significance of feedback loops, mutualistic relationships, and holism in ensuring effective governance.

Implementation Plan:

A step-by-step guide to actualizing the nature-inspired blueprint is presented, covering critical aspects such as the establishment of a Coalition Council, transparency mechanisms, accountability frameworks, conflict resolution, stability measures, public engagement, and periodic reviews. The plan provides tangible strategies to navigate the complexities of coalition governance, ensuring long-term sustainability.

Conclusion:

By emulating nature's timeless wisdom, political landscapes can be transformed into a harmonious, collaborative, and effective system. This nature-inspired coalition agreement is more than just a blueprint for governance; it represents a vision for a united, prosperous, and resilient nation.

OUTLINE

Chapter 1: Introduction to Biomimicry in Politics

Nature is a master innovator. Through billions of years of evolution, it has developed strategies, designs, and systems that humans can only aspire to emulate. Biomimicry is the practice of drawing inspiration from these natural designs to solve human problems. In the realm of politics, biomimicry offers a lens through which we can envision a world where collaboration, balance, and mutual respect reign supreme.

Chapter 2: Keystone Species: Nature's Pillars of Balance

Keystone species are those that have a disproportionately large effect on their environment relative to their abundance. Their presence and actions dictate the health and balance of entire ecosystems. By examining ecosystems such as the tropical rainforests, coral reefs, grasslands, and wetlands, we uncover the harmonious interplay of various keystone species. These species, whether they are elephants, jaguars, parrotfish, bison, or beavers, teach us the importance of shared responsibility, symbiotic relationships, and mutual respect.

Chapter 3: The Lessons from Nature: Applying Biomimicry Principles in Political Coalitions

Drawing parallels between nature's keystone species and political entities, we can derive essential principles:

- **Resource Regulation and Distribution**: Equitable sharing of power and responsibilities based on representation.

- **Balanced Predation**: A system of checks and balances to prevent dominance by any single party.

- **Habitat Creation and Modification**: Encouraging collaborative projects and initiatives for the greater good.

- **Symbiotic Relationships**: Forging policy partnerships and shared platforms for mutual benefit.

- **Disease and Pest Regulation**: Ensuring transparency, oversight, and accountability in governance.

Chapter 4: Principles for a Blueprint for Collaborative Governance

Inspired by the lessons from nature, this chapter delves deep into crafting an agreement that political parties can adopt. It emphasizes equitable distribution, shared decision-making, rotating leadership, policy partnerships, and robust mechanisms for transparency and accountability. This blueprint is more than just a guide; it represents a vision for a united nation, drawing strength from its diversity.

Chapter 5: Implementing the Nature-Inspired Blueprint for Collaborative Governance in Political Frameworks

Having a blueprint is just the beginning. This chapter provides a step-by-Implementing the Nature-Inspired Blueprint for Collaborative Governance in Political Frameworks, focusing on the establishment of a central Coalition Council, transparency mechanisms, an accountability framework, conflict resolution systems, stability measures, public engagement strategies, and periodic reviews and renewals. Each step is carefully crafted, keeping in mind the overarching principles of fairness, transparency, and collaboration.

Chapter 6: The Ripple Effect: Recognizing and Harnessing Interconnectedness for adaptive Coalition Governance

Nature is a tapestry of complexity, intricately woven with interdependencies. From the tiniest microorganism to the grandest mammal, each entity plays a role that impacts the larger ecosystem. This chapter seeks to explore the concept of the "ripple effect" in nature and its implications for collaborative governance. By recognizing and harnessing these interconnections, a coalition government can achieve synergy, resilience, and long-term sustainability.

DEDICATION

May this book serve as a beacon, guiding nations towards a future where politics is not just about power, but about service, collaboration, and the greater good. In the dance of keystone species, in the harmony of ecosystems, lies the promise of a brighter tomorrow.

May the journey this book it inspires, be a testament to the enduring spirit of citizens striving towards unity in diversity, strength in collaboration, and prosperity in shared purpose. Let us step into this new dawn with the wisdom of the past, the knowledge of the present, and the hope for a brighter future.

ACKNOWLEDGMENTS

Special thanks to the diverse ecosystems of our planet that continue to inspire and teach us every day. To the citizens, may you always find strength in unity and diversity.

CONTENTS

Introduction to Biomimicry in Politics

In the vast expanse of the universe, Earth stands out as a beacon of life, a marvel of biodiversity and interdependent systems. From the microscopic to the macroscopic, nature presents a symphony of life, each note playing a crucial role in the composition. At the heart of this symphony lies an age-old principle - biomimicry.

Derived from the Greek words, 'bios' meaning life and 'mimesis' meaning imitation, biomimicry is about understanding and emulating nature's strategies to address human challenges. For eons, nature has been perfecting designs, processes, and systems that exhibit optimal efficiency, resilience, and sustainability. Instead of reinventing the wheel, biomimicry suggests that humanity can find answers to its pressing challenges by looking to nature's tried and tested solutions.

Take, for example, the intricate design of a spider's web. This marvel of engineering is not only structurally sound, but also highly efficient in capturing prey. Remarkably, when comparing its strength on a kilogram-for-kilogram basis, spider silk is found to be stronger than Kevlar, the material commonly used in bulletproof vests. Engineers and architects, inspired by this natural design, have been studying the spider's web properties to create stronger yet lighter materials.

Similarly, the way certain plants in arid regions conserve water have inspired innovative water management solutions in drought-prone areas. But biomimicry is not just limited to engineering or architecture. Its principles can be applied across various domains, including the realm of politics.

But how does this apply to politics? How can we draw inspiration from nature to foster collaboration and create a blueprint for collaborative governance?

Politics, at its core, is about governance and ensuring the well-being of a nation's citizens. It involves decision-making, resource allocation, conflict resolution, and setting the direction for the future. Yet, in today's polarized world, politics often becomes a battleground of ideologies, where collaboration takes a backseat, and power struggles become the norm.

In nature, we have Keystone species, organisms that play a critical and unique role in the way their ecosystem functions. Without these species, the ecosystem would be drastically different or cease to function altogether. Take the African elephant as an example. These majestic creatures are keystone species due to their substantial impact on their environment. African elephants help maintain savanna and forest ecosystems by controlling the growth of certain plants and trees through their feeding habits. By uprooting trees and trampling vegetation, they create space for smaller plants to grow, which in turn supports a wider range of wildlife. Additionally, their dung is a crucial nutrient source and helps in seed dispersal, aiding in plant reproduction across vast areas. The benefits provided by the African elephant extend beyond just ecological balance. They also play a significant role in shaping the landscape, which can affect local climate and water cycles.

Similarly, in politics, we have keystone species known as politicians who hold immense power and influence over governance. They are responsible for decision-making processes that shape the future of nations. Just as keystone species maintain ecological balance by their presence or absence in an ecosystem, politicians have the ability to shape political landscapes through their actions or lack thereof.

Can the world of politics learn from the collaborative and balanced interactions of keystone species in an ecosystem? The answer is a resounding yes. Think about a mature forest ecosystem. Here, trees, shrubs, herbivores, carnivores, insects, fungi, and microbes coexist. Each entity plays a role, and there is a balance of power. No single species can dominate without causing disruption. Trees provide shelter and food, herbivores keep certain plants in check, carnivores ensure herbivores do not overpopulate, and fungi decompose, recycling nutrients back into the soil. There's competition, but there's also collaboration. There is a system of checks and balances that ensures the health and longevity of the forest.

Translating this to the political landscape, there is a need for a system where multiple parties can coexist, contribute, and collaborate. Instead of one-party monopolizing power, there is a shared responsibility, where decisions are made collectively, considering diverse perspectives. Just as in nature, where the loss of one species can disrupt an entire ecosystem, in politics, marginalizing or suppressing one party or community can lead to unrest and instability. Just as nature's keystone species collaborate with other organisms for the benefit of their ecosystems, politicians must work together to optimize developmental outcomes for the entire population.

Biomimicry in politics is about fostering a culture of mutual respect, understanding, and shared purpose. It is about recognizing that each party, irrespective of its size or influence, brings something unique to the table. It is about moving away from power struggles and zero-sum games and moving towards consensus-building, dialogue, and shared vision.

But how can these principles be practically applied? How can political parties, with their distinct ideologies and priorities, come together for the greater good? These are questions that this book aims to address in the subsequent chapters.

In conclusion, biomimicry offers a fresh perspective on politics, emphasizing collaboration over confrontation, mutual benefit over individual gain, and long-term vision over short-term gains. As we delve deeper into the principles of biomimicry and explore their application in the political landscape, let us keep an open mind, recognizing that nature, with its millions of years of wisdom, might just have the answers we seek.

Keystone Species: Nature's Pillars of Balance

In the grand theatre of nature, every species plays a role, contributing to the narrative of life. However, amidst this vast ensemble, certain species stand out, not because of their abundance or dominance, but because of the pivotal roles they play in maintaining the stability and health of their ecosystems. These are the keystone species, the linchpins that hold the intricate web of life together.

The term 'keystone species' draws inspiration from the central wedge-shaped stone in an arch, the keystone, which holds all other stones in place. Remove the keystone, and the arch collapses. Similarly, in an ecosystem, the removal or significant reduction of a keystone species results in a cascade of changes, often leading to a dramatic shift in the composition and health of the system.

But what makes these species so integral to their environments? Let us delve deeper into the world of keystone species to understand their significance and the lessons they offer.

1. The Role of Resource Regulation and Distribution

In the dense rainforests of South America, the jaguar reigns supreme. As an apex predator, it keeps herbivore populations in check, preventing overgrazing and ensuring a balanced distribution of resources. However, the jaguar's role does not end there. Its hunting patterns influence the behaviour of its prey, affecting where they feed, how they move, and even their reproductive strategies. Through these intricate interactions, the jaguar helps shape the very structure and composition of the rainforest.

Similarly, in the political realm, certain entities such as political parties or institutions can play a crucial role in regulating resources and ensuring their fair distribution. They set the tone for collaboration, influence patterns of behaviour, and shape the broader landscape.

2. Habitat Creation and Modification

Beavers, often dubbed as nature's engineers, are known for their dam-building behaviour. By constructing dams across streams, they create wetlands – habitats that benefit a multitude of species, from amphibians and fish to birds and plants. The wetlands store water, recharge groundwater, and function as natural filters. Additionally, these wetlands contribute significantly to flood attenuation by absorbing excess flood water like a sponge and then releasing it slowly, mitigating the impacts of flooding in surrounding areas. In the absence of beavers, these habitats would drastically reduce, affecting all dependent species.

Drawing a parallel to governance, certain policies or initiatives can create or modify 'habitats' – opportunities and environments that benefit various segments of society. Just as beavers transform landscapes, visionary political leadership can reshape nations, creating opportunities and fostering environments where diverse communities thrive. Through their actions and policies, they construct political habitats that promote inclusivity, social justice, economic prosperity, and sustainable development. It is through these transformative actions that they contribute to the overall health and resilience of the political ecosystem.

3. Balancing Acts and Symbiotic Relationships

In the vibrant coral reefs, the parrotfish plays a seemingly simple yet vital role. By grazing on the algae that grow on corals, they prevent the corals from being overwhelmed, ensuring the reef's health. At the same time, cleaner fish, like the cleaner wrasse, form symbiotic relationships with larger fish, picking off parasites for food and ensuring the health of the bigger fish. This balance of roles and mutualistic relationships is essential for the vitality of coral reefs.

In a coalition government, parties can form symbiotic relationships, supporting and complementing each other's strengths and weaknesses. Just as the parrotfish and cleaner wrasse play distinct but interdependent roles, political parties can collaborate, ensuring the health and balance of governance.

4. Disease and Pest Regulation

Frogs and other amphibians, often overlooked in their importance, play a vital role in controlling insect populations. By feeding on mosquitoes and other pests, they help regulate diseases and ensure a balance in their ecosystems. Their presence or absence can serve as an indicator of the health of their environment.

In the realm of politics, regulatory bodies and oversight committees play a similar role, keeping 'pests' – such as corruption, unethical practices, or mismanagement – in check. Their initiative-taking actions ensure a healthy environment for democratic processes and good governance.

5. The Ripple Effect

The influence of keystone species often extends beyond their immediate environment. For instance, the presence of wolves in North American forests affects the behaviour of deer, reducing overgrazing. This, in turn, allows vegetation to recover, affecting everything from the soil composition to the bird species that inhabit the area. The ripple effect of a single keystone species is profound, shaping entire ecosystems.

Similarly, in a coalition governance system, the actions of one party can have cascading effects on the entire political landscape. Decisions made, alliances formed, or policies implemented can influence public opinion, shape national narratives, and impact future collaborations. Furthermore, the actions of one political party can create ripples that impact not only policy outcomes but also societal perceptions and attitudes towards governance.

In conclusion, keystone species serve as a testament to the interconnectedness of life. Their roles, while often subtle, are pivotal in maintaining the balance and health of their ecosystems. They teach us the importance of understanding and valuing every player in a system, recognizing that each contributes to the broader narrative.

In the subsequent chapters, as we explore how the principles observed in keystone species can be applied to the political landscape, let us remember that nature's wisdom offers more than just strategies. It offers a vision of harmony, collaboration, and mutual respect — a vision that, if embraced, can transform the future of a nation.

The Lessons from Nature:

Applying Biomimicry Principles in Political Coalitions

Nature is often romanticised for its serene landscapes and poetic harmonies. Yet beneath this tranquil facade lies a dynamic world of complex relationships, intricate balances, and strategic collaborations. These phenomena, which have evolved over millennia, offer profound insights that can be applied to modern political systems, especially in the challenging realm of coalition governance. In this chapter, we will delve into the core principles derived from nature's playbook and explore how they can shape and strengthen political coalitions.

1. The Principle of Resource Regulation and Distribution

In the vast savannahs of Africa, a delicate balance exists among the diverse inhabitants. Predators, despite their prowess, do not decimate prey populations. Grazers, although numerous, do not exhaust grasslands. This balance ensures the ecosystem remains vibrant and diverse. Nature teaches us that unchecked dominance or overexploitation leads to systemic collapse.

Political Application: In a coalition, resources – whether they are ministerial positions, mayoral committee positions, budgetary allocations, or policy influence – need equitable distribution. Parties, irrespective of their size, should have a voice and representation. This prevents monopolization, encourages collaboration, and fosters a sense of shared responsibility. Just as in nature, where resource regulation ensures ecosystem health, in politics, it ensures coalition stability.

2. The Dance of Balanced Predation

Nature is full of examples where predators and prey coexist in a delicate balance. In the African savannah, the interaction between lions and zebras exemplifies this balance. Lions hunt zebras for food, but this predation also keeps the zebra population in check, averting overgrazing and maintaining the health of the savannah ecosystem.

Political Application: In a coalition government, the concept of "balanced predation" translates to checks and balances. While one party might champion a particular policy or initiative, others have the right to review, suggest modifications, or may even have ability to veto if a consensus is not achieved. This ensures that no single party or policy becomes too dominant, maintaining a balance of power and influence.

3. Collaborative Habitat Creation and Modification

Mangrove forests, found in coastal regions, are nature's defence against erosion and storm surges. These forests, with their intricate root systems, not only protect coastlines but also provide habitats for a myriad of species. They represent a symbiotic environment where various species benefit from the habitat's existence.

Political Application: In the realm of coalition politics, "habitat creation" can be likened to the creation of inclusive policies and platforms that benefit a wide array of societal segments. Collaborative projects, be they infrastructural, educational, or health-oriented, should be jointly overseen by coalition parties, ensuring diverse perspectives and shared responsibility. In some jurisdictions this may already be enshrined in the governance system, but not optimally implemented.

4. The Symphony of Symbiotic Relationships

The African savannah showcases a fascinating symbiotic relationship between oxpeckers and large herbivores like buffalo. Oxpeckers feed on ticks and other parasites found on buffalo, providing a cleaning service to the herbivores while obtaining food for themselves. This mutualistic relationship benefits both parties involved.

Political Application: Coalition parties can form similar symbiotic relationships, leveraging each other's strengths and compensating for weaknesses. By pooling resources, knowledge, and expertise, parties can jointly address national challenges, whether they pertain to the economy, healthcare, education, or security. Through these partnerships, parties can ensure broader consensus and holistic policymaking.

5. Guardians of Disease and Pest Regulation

In many ecosystems, specific species play roles in regulating disease vectors or pests. Birds, bats, and dragonflies, for instance, play a crucial role in controlling mosquito populations, thus keeping diseases like malaria in check.

Political Application: In the political landscape, "disease and pest regulation" can be equated with the regulation of corruption, inefficiencies, and unethical practices. Independent oversight bodies, watchdogs, and transparency mechanisms are vital to monitor, report, and address any malpractices within the coalition. Regular audits, public disclosures, and feedback mechanisms ensure the coalition remains transparent, accountable, and responsive to the people's needs.

6. The Ripple Effect: Understanding Interconnectedness

In a freshwater pond, the presence or absence of a single species, like the dragonfly, can influence the entire ecosystem. Dragonflies feed on mosquitoes, preventing their overpopulation. Without dragonflies, mosquito populations could explode, leading to potential disease outbreaks and affecting the pond's overall health.

Political Application: Every decision, policy, or action taken by a coalition party has ripple effects throughout the political and societal spectrum. Recognizing this interconnectedness is crucial. Parties must understand the broader implications of their actions, ensuring that decisions made are in the best interest of the nation and its diverse populace.

In conclusion, nature, with its millennia of evolutionary wisdom, provides a roadmap for effective, balanced, and collaborative governance. By understanding and emulating these principles, political coalitions can navigate the complexities of governance, ensuring stability, inclusivity, and progress. Embracing these lessons from nature could pave the way for a harmonious, prosperous, and united future.

Principles for a Blueprint for Collaborative Governance

Many countries embarking on political coalitions have a rich tapestry of cultures, languages, and histories, presenting different layers of complexity on the road to transformation. As any nation moves into an era of coalition governance, there is both an opportunity and a challenge. The opportunity lies in harnessing the diverse strengths of multiple parties for the greater good, while the challenge is to navigate the complexities of shared governance, ensuring stability, inclusivity, and progress.

Drawing inspiration from nature's wisdom, especially the principles observed in keystone species and their ecosystems, this chapter presents a comprehensive blueprint for collaborative governance.

1. Embracing the Principle of Equitable Distribution

Nature thrives on balance. From the lush rainforests of the Amazon to the arid deserts of the Sahara, resources are distributed in a manner that sustains life, allowing diverse species to coexist and flourish.

Political Application: In a coalition government, there is a need for an equitable distribution of power, resources, and responsibilities. This means ensuring that ministerial positions, mayoral committee positions, policy influences, and budgetary allocations are proportionally distributed based on the representation and strength of each party in the coalition.

This fosters a sense of belonging, minimizes power struggles, and ensures that every voice is heard.

2. Nurturing the Dance of Balanced Predation

In ecosystems, the balance between predators and prey is essential for stability. Neither can dominate without causing disruption. This balance ensures diversity and resilience.

Political Application: In the realm of politics, the concept of 'balanced predation' translates to checks and balances. Rotating leadership roles, shared responsibilities, and periodic reviews ensure that no single party or ideology dominates. A system where leadership roles rotate among coalition partners ensures diversity in decision-making and prevents any single party's prolonged dominance.

The opportunities (such as role and duration) to lead may be based on the representation of each party in the coalition and subject to the benefitting party having a person who meets minimum defined criteria to play a particular role. For example, if a role requires a person with financial literacy, it would not be prudent to give leadership to a person who lacks such capacity just for the sake of equitable rotation.

3. Fostering Collaborative Habitat Creation

Nature thrives on collaboration. Be it the symbiotic relationship between bees and flowers or the intricate interplay between predators and prey, collaboration is the bedrock of thriving ecosystems.

Political Application: Coalition governments should prioritize collaborative projects and initiatives. Joint task forces, comprising members from all coalition parties, can be established to address pressing national issues. These collaborative endeavours ensure that policies and projects are holistic, benefitting from the diverse expertise and perspectives of different parties.

For example, joint task teams comprising members from all coalition parties can co-create solutions with beneficiary communities on contentious issues such as land allocation and transparency in the award of development tenders.

4. Building Strong Symbiotic Relationships

In the African savannah, the relationship between oxpeckers and buffalo showcases the power of symbiosis. Such relationships, built on mutual benefit, are integral to nature's balance.

Political Application: Political parties, each with its strengths, weaknesses, and areas of expertise, can form symbiotic relationships. These partnerships, built on mutual respect and shared objectives, can lead to more comprehensive and inclusive policies.

Shared platforms can be established where parties collaborate, bringing together their resources, knowledge, and expertise for the nation's benefit. Imagine how coalition partners could foster social cohesion in their communities if they could conduct regular joint "Town Hall" meetings, with all political party representatives and their supporters interacting in one meeting.

5. Vigilance in Disease and Pest Regulation

Nature has its guardians. From birds that keep insect populations in check to fungi that decompose and recycle nutrients, these guardians ensure the health and balance of their ecosystems.

Political Application: Guardianship in a coalition translates to mechanisms that ensure transparency, accountability, and integrity. Independent oversight bodies and watchdogs play a crucial role in monitoring and addressing any instances of corruption, unethical practices, or mismanagement.

Regular audits, coupled with transparent public disclosures, ensure that the coalition remains accountable to the people. The electorate should be empowered to hold their political representatives accountable, including dissolving the coalition if the collective if not serving the interests of the community. For example, social audits can be conducted for each project, comprising local political leadership, technocrats and community leaders.

The objective would be to complement the Auditor General who may focus on financial compliance whilst the social audits focus on confirming project deliverables were achieved.

In line with empowering the electorate to be involved in the development agenda and hold politicians accountable, it is proposed to the establish digital platforms for real-time feedback. These platforms will enable citizens to actively participate in policy-making processes and provide valuable insights and perspectives.

By embracing technology and creating avenues for direct engagement, politicians can ensure that decision-making is informed by the diverse voices of the people they represent. This approach strengthens democratic principles and fosters a sense of ownership among citizens.

6. Recognizing the Ripple Effect

Every action in nature has consequences, often extending beyond immediate surroundings. The flutter of a butterfly's wings can, metaphorically, set off a tornado miles away.

Political Application: Every decision made by a coalition party has implications that ripple through the political, social, and economic fabric of the nation. Recognizing this interconnectedness, parties must engage in thorough deliberations before making decisions. This ensures that decisions are holistic, taking into account the broader implications and potential consequences.

7. Embracing Adaptability

Nature is dynamic. Species evolve, ecosystems adapt, and life finds a way even in the most challenging circumstances.

Political Application: A coalition government, much like a living ecosystem, needs to be adaptable. Regular reviews, feedback mechanisms, and open channels of communication among coalition partners ensure that the coalition remains responsive to the changing needs and aspirations of the nation. Any changes should benefit the affected communities and not to entrench self-interests and political power of individual parties or the coalition as a collective.

It is essential to understand that the intention of this book is not to render politicians irrelevant or powerless. On the contrary, politicians play a vital role as catalysts for change in our society. By fostering collaboration among themselves and between politicians and the electorate, they can optimize developmental outcomes for the entire population.

In conclusion, this blueprint, inspired by nature's timeless wisdom, offers a roadmap for collaborative governance. It emphasizes the principles of equity, collaboration, transparency, adaptability, and mutual respect. As the nation embarks on this journey of coalition governance, the lessons from nature serve as guiding stars, illuminating a path towards a harmonious and prosperous future. It is a journey that requires patience, understanding, and a shared vision, but with nature as our guide, the destination promises a united and thriving nation.

Implementing the Nature-Inspired Blueprint for Collaborative Governance in Political Frameworks

Having drawn inspiration from the intricate designs and collaborative strategies of nature, the next pivotal step is to implement these lessons in the political realm. But how can we translate these principles into actionable strategies? How can we ensure that the blueprint does not merely remain a theoretical concept but evolves into a tangible framework that reshapes the nation's political landscape? This chapter aims to provide a detailed, step-by-step guide to actualizing the nature-inspired blueprint for collaborative governance.

1. Establishment of the Coalition Council: The Heartbeat of Collaboration

Nature thrives on interconnected systems. The roots of trees connect with fungi to form mycorrhizal networks, facilitating nutrient exchange and communication amongst trees.

Political Application: A Coalition Council should be established as the central body to oversee the functioning of the coalition. This council will:

- Comprise representatives from all coalition parties, ensuring diverse representation.

- Meet regularly to review progress, address challenges, and strategize for the future.

- Manage the pace of transformation including the necessary changes in policies and regulatory frameworks.

- Serve as a mediation platform, resolving disputes and fostering understanding among parties.

2. Transparency Mechanism: The Clear Waters of Governance

Clear waters in a stream signify health, purity, and vitality. Similarly, transparency is the lifeblood of a trustworthy government.

Political Application: A robust transparency mechanism should be instituted:

- Develop digital platforms, such as user-friendly websites and apps, where citizens can access real-time information about coalition activities, decisions, and expenditures.

- Implement feedback systems, where the public can voice opinions, concerns, and suggestions, ensuring the government remains responsive.

- Regularly disclose major decisions, policies, and actions to the public through press releases, media briefings, and digital platforms.

3. Accountability Framework: The Regulating Forces of Nature

In nature, every entity is accountable for its actions. A predator that overhunts risks food scarcity, while a tree that overshadows might deprive other plants of sunlight.

Political Application: An accountability framework ensures that every action taken by the coalition is for the nation's greater good:

- Agree on how the coalition will be managed and its performance evaluated. This should be done before elections.

- Conduct periodic performance reviews, assessing the coalition's achievements and areas for improvement.

- Institute independent audits to evaluate the coalition's activities, finances, and decisions.

- Establish corrective measures to rectify any shortcomings or challenges identified during reviews and audits.

4. Conflict Resolution Mechanism: Nature's Equilibrium

Nature has its conflicts, from territorial disputes among animals to competition for sunlight among plants. Yet, it always finds equilibrium.

Political Application: Conflicts in a coalition are inevitable, but can be managed through:

- A dedicated Conflict Resolution Committee comprising neutral members from each party.

- External mediation when conflicts cannot be internally resolved.

- Binding arbitration for conflicts that remain unresolved, ensuring decisions are respected by all parties.

5. Stability Measures: The Resilient Foundations of Nature

From the deep roots of trees that prevent soil erosion to the mutualistic relationships between species, nature builds resilient systems. Periodic cycles of self-renewal enhance the ecosystem.

Political Application: To ensure the coalition's stability:

- Organize regular coalition retreats, fostering team building, mutual understanding, and strategic planning.

- Engage with the public regularly, ensuring that the coalition remains grounded in the needs and aspirations of the people.

- Agree a framework for the electorate to conduct a vote of no confidence and dissolve a dysfunctional coalition. It should be easy for the electorate to know who has shortcomings.

- Implement a moratorium on votes of no confidence for a specified period, allowing the coalition to establish itself and conduct its mandate.

6. Public Engagement: Nature's Web of Interconnections

Every entity in nature is interconnected, from the pollinators to the plants they pollinate. Furthermore, organisms such as bees and ants can teach us about decentralized decision-making.

Political Application: A successful coalition remains deeply connected with the people it serves:

- Organize town hall meetings in various regions, fostering direct interaction between the public and coalition representatives.

- Use digital platforms and public forums to gather feedback from citizens on policies, initiatives, and decisions.

- Use participatory budgeting processes that reflect decentralized decision-making.

- Ensure that the coalition remains responsive, adapting to feedback and addressing the public's concerns.

7. Review and Renewal: Nature's Cycle of Evolution

Nature is in a constant state of evolution, adapting to changes, and renewing itself.

Political Application: The coalition agreement should be dynamic, reflecting the changing political and social landscape:

- Conduct annual reviews of the coalition agreement to assess its relevance and effectiveness.

- Allow parties to renegotiate terms based on changing scenarios and needs without compromising the principles of transparency, accountability, equity, and fairness.

- Implement necessary amendments to the agreement, ensuring it remains a living document that evolves with time.

In conclusion, the implementation of the nature-inspired blueprint is a journey that requires commitment, collaboration, and a deep understanding of the principles that have sustained ecosystems for millennia. By taking these actionable steps, citizens can pave the way for a coalition governance model that stands as a testament to the nation's resilience, diversity, and shared vision for a brighter future. With nature as the guiding compass, the nation can embark on a transformative journey towards harmonious, inclusive, and effective governance.

The Ripple Effect: Recognizing and Harnessing Interconnectedness for Adaptive Coalition Governance

Nature is a tapestry of complexity, intricately woven with interdependencies. From the tiniest microorganism to the grandest mammal, each entity plays a role that impacts the larger ecosystem. This chapter seeks to explore the concept of the "ripple effect" in nature and its implications for collaborative governance. By recognizing and harnessing these interconnections, a coalition government can achieve synergy, resilience, and long-term sustainability.

1. Nature's Symphony of Interconnectedness

In the lush rainforests, when a tree falls, it creates an opening in the canopy that allows sunlight to reach the forest floor. This sudden influx of light triggers an explosion of growth among plants previously overshadowed. Similarly, the disappearance of a predator can lead to an overpopulation of certain species, disrupting the balance of the ecosystem.

Political Application: In the political realm, the actions or inactions of one party can have cascading effects on the entire coalition and the nation at large. It is imperative to recognize this inherent interconnectedness as every policy decision, alliance formed, or public statement made has far-reaching consequences on political landscapes as well as social and economic spheres.

2. The Butterfly Effect: Small Actions, Profound Outcomes

The 'butterfly effect' suggests that the flap of a butterfly's wings in Brazil can set off a tornado in Texas. Though metaphorical, it emphasizes the profound impact of seemingly minor actions.

Political Application: In a coalition, even minor decisions or statements by one party can have significant implications for the entire coalition. It is vital for parties to communicate, deliberate, and ensure that their individual actions align with the coalition's collective objectives. Small missteps, if not addressed, can escalate into major challenges.

3. Mutualistic Relationships: Building upon Shared Strengths

In nature, mutualistic relationships, such as those between bees and flowering plants, result in win-win scenarios. Bees get nectar, and plants get pollinated.

Political Application: For a coalition to thrive, parties must foster mutualistic relationships. By leveraging each other's strengths, sharing resources, and collaborating on joint initiatives, parties can achieve outcomes that would be challenging to accomplish individually. Such partnerships not only strengthen the coalition but also lead to holistic and inclusive policies that benefit the nation.

4. Feedback Loops: Nature's System of Checks and Balances

Nature operates through feedback loops. When a population grows too large, food scarcity or increased predation restores balance. These feedback mechanisms ensure stability and equilibrium.

Political Application: Feedback loops are crucial in a coalition setting. Regular reviews, public consultations, and intra-coalition dialogues provide insights into the coalition's performance and areas for improvement. By actively seeking and acting upon feedback, the coalition can adapt, evolve, and address challenges proactively.

5. Redundancy and Resilience: Lessons from Nature's Design

Ecosystems often have multiple species performing similar roles, ensuring that if one species is impacted, others can maintain the system's function. This redundancy enhances resilience.

Political Application: In a coalition, it is beneficial to have shared responsibilities and overlapping roles. If one party faces internal challenges or is unable to fulfil a particular responsibility, others can step in, ensuring continuity and stability in governance.

For example, if a party is offered a rotational role, but lacks expertise to perform the role, it should be normal to defer the opportunity to someone from another party who is capable to deliver on behalf of the entire coalition.

6. Adaptation and Evolution: Nature's Response to Change

Nature is dynamic, constantly adapting to changes. Species evolve, ecosystems transition, and life finds a way to thrive amid challenges.

Political Application: A coalition government, too, must be adaptable. As the political landscape shifts, societal needs evolve, or global scenarios change, the coalition must be ready to adapt its strategies, policies, and priorities. This adaptability ensures that the government remains relevant, responsive, and effective in addressing the nation's ever-evolving needs.

However, adapting to evolving changes should not be used to advance the interests of some coalition members at the expense of others and the electorate. The best time to effect major changes is before elections.

7. The Principle of Holism: Seeing the Bigger Picture

In nature, the whole is often greater than the sum of its parts. An ecosystem's health is not merely a function of individual species, but results from their collective interactions and relationships.

Political Application: A coalition government embodies holism. While individual parties bring their strengths, ideologies, and priorities to the table, the coalition's success lies in its ability to integrate these diverse elements into a cohesive, united, and effective governance strategy. Recognizing and harnessing this holistic potential can elevate the coalition's impact, driving transformative change for the nation.

In conclusion, the ripple effect, as observed in nature, offers profound insights for coalition governance. By understanding, recognizing, and harnessing the intricate interconnections inherent in the political landscape, a coalition government can navigate challenges, seize opportunities, and chart a course towards a harmonious, prosperous, and sustainable future. Embracing the lessons from nature's intricate web of interdependencies can transform challenges into opportunities, turning the coalition's diversity into its greatest strength.

Epilogue: Reflecting on the Nature of Coalitions

This book has journeyed through the lush fields of nature's wisdom, seeking to draw parallels between the harmonious symphony of ecosystems and the potential for collaborative governance.

We began our exploration by delving into the concept of biomimicry in politics, unravelling the intricate designs and strategies nature employs to sustain life. Through the lens of keystone species, we observed the delicate balance of ecosystems, where every entity, regardless of its size or prominence, plays a crucial role in maintaining the health and vitality of the whole.

Drawing inspiration from these natural phenomena, we proposed a new paradigm for political coalitions. A paradigm where power and responsibilities are equitably distributed, where diverse voices are not just heard but actively shape decisions, and where transparency and accountability are not mere ideals but the bedrock of governance.

Our journey led us to craft a comprehensive blueprint for collaborative governance, emphasizing principles such as balanced predation, collaborative habitat creation, symbiotic relationships, and the ripple effect of interconnectedness. We envisioned a political ecosystem where parties, like the diverse species in nature, coexist, collaborate, and contribute to the nation's prosperity.

Implementing this transformative blueprint necessitates commitment, patience, and an unwavering dedication to equity, transparency, and mutual respect. I outlined actionable steps, from the establishment of a Coalition Council to public engagement strategies, ensuring that the coalition remains dynamic, responsive, and grounded in the needs of the people.

My proposal emphasizes empowering the electorate to be involved in the development agenda and holding politicians accountable through various structures and mechanisms for planning, oversight, and conflict resolution. By involving the people directly in decision-making processes, we foster collaboration between politicians and citizens, optimizing developmental outcomes for everyone.

Moreover, there are skeptics who question whether politicians will ever allow a change to the status quo. It is crucial to clarify that our intention is not to render politicians irrelevant or powerless. On the contrary, they have a pivotal role akin to keystone species in maintaining balance and health within our political ecosystem. Collaboration among politicians themselves as well as between politicians and citizens is essential for achieving optimal outcomes for all.

Furthermore, some may argue that incorporating these proposals into existing legislation would take centuries. However, it is important to note that our proposals are not intended for slow piecemeal implementation over an extended period. Instead, they call for transformational changes within the political system itself—a swift adoption of new governance models inspired by nature's resilience and adaptability.

As we stand at the threshold of a new era of coalition governance, it is imperative to remember that the path ahead, though filled with challenges, also brims with opportunities. Opportunities to redefine politics, to transform the way decisions are made, and to forge a future where diverse perspectives are not just tolerated but celebrated.

Transparency, accountability, equity, and fairness are crucial elements in any successful coalition. Crafting proper measures to ensure these principles are upheld is essential in preventing power struggles. When politicians know they are accountable to the voters who put their trust in them, they have a greater incentive to collaborate rather than engage in self-serving behaviours.

Just as in the vibrant ecosystems of our planet, where diversity breeds strength and resilience, our political landscape thrives on the diverse voices and perspectives of multiple parties. The coalition is not just an agreement of convenience; it is a commitment to unity, transparency, and the greater good. It represents a shift from the politics of dominance to a politics of collaboration, where every voice is valued, every perspective is considered, and every decision is made for the benefit of the entire nation.

Political parties are urged to agree criteria for contentious issues such as the Coalition Council membership, rotation of leadership, monitoring and evaluation mechanisms and structures well ahead of elections. This would enhance objectivity that would otherwise be compromised by self-interests if the exercise were conducted post elections.

A coalition is a commitment to unity, transparency, and the greater good. It represents a shift from the politics of dominance to a politics of collaboration, where every voice is valued, every perspective is considered, and every decision is made for the benefit of the entire nation.

In this envisioned future, I see coalitions not as battlegrounds of conflicting interests, but as fertile grounds for innovative solutions born from collaborative efforts. I see nations where the electorate, empowered and informed, plays an active role in holding its leaders accountable, akin to nature's own checks and balances.

This epilogue is not merely a conclusion but a clarion call to action, beckoning us to step into a world where political entities, like the diverse species of the savannah, coexist in mutual respect and collaborative purpose. Let us step forward, inspired and guided by nature's timeless wisdom, to create a political symphony that resonates with the heartbeat of our nation just like the intricate symphony of the African savannah.

The path ahead will be challenging, as all journeys of change are. But with nature as our guide, we can navigate these challenges with wisdom and grace. We can transform our political landscape into a vibrant, thriving ecosystem of ideas, collaboration, and progress.

In the words of Nelson Mandela, "It always seems impossible until it's done." As the night falls on the African savannah, let us look to the stars for guidance and inspiration. Let us forge a future where our political coalitions are as harmonious and resilient as the symphony of life that surrounds us. For in the harmony of ecosystems lies the blueprint for a united, prosperous, and resilient nation.

Simulation Skit: A Biomimicry Workshop for The ABC Metro Council

Day 1: The Intricate Dance of Coalition Politics

In the well-furnished chamber of the newly formed ABC Metro Council, a diverse group of politicians gathered, their faces a mixture of curiosity and cautious optimism. The air buzzed with the undercurrents of recent electoral tensions, where no party had managed to secure a definitive majority to lead the process of setting up governance structures. This first meeting was crucial, aimed at negotiating a coalition agreement to govern the city. The setting was ripe with the potential for conflict and cooperation, mirroring the complexity of a newly formed ecosystem.

At the head of the room stood Mr. Gama, a renowned biomimicry practitioner, invited by the City Manager to facilitate a series of workshops. His task was monumental yet simple in its aim: to guide these politicians through the principles of biomimicry to foster a collaborative environment conducive to sustainable governance.

"Welcome, everyone," Mr. Gama began, his voice calm yet resonant, capturing the room's attention. "Over the next week, we are not merely forming a coalition; we are attempting to emulate nature's wisdom in governance. Nature, through its billions of years of evolution, has perfected the art of collaboration, resilience, and sustainability."

The room, filled with a palpable mix of eagerness and skepticism, listened as Mr. Gama continued. "Consider the African savannah—a place where diverse species coexist and thrive not despite their differences but because of them. Each species plays a critical role, much like each of your parties will hopefully do in this council."

The mention of the savannah stirred a murmur among the councillors, particularly the smaller party representatives, who often felt overshadowed by the larger factions.

Mr. Gama proposed an exercise. "Let's start with a simple task. Each of you will share one key strength that your party can bring to this coalition, much like how each animal in the savannah contributes to the ecosystem's health."

One by one, the politicians spoke. The larger parties touted their experienced leadership and policy expertise, while the smaller groups highlighted unique local insights and innovative problem-solving strategies.

However, tensions rose when discussing leadership roles within the coalition. The larger parties expected to dominate these positions, while the smaller parties protested, citing the need for equitable representation.

Seeing the brewing storm, Mr. Gama introduced a concept from his biomimicry toolkit. "Let's consider the role of keystone species in an ecosystem. These species, although not always the most numerous, have an outsized impact on their environment. Their activities promote a rich diversity, which enhances the resilience of the ecosystem."

He continued, "In our context, each party, regardless of size, should have the opportunity to lead in areas where they have expertise, ensuring a balanced and effective governance model."

The suggestion was met with mixed reactions. A seasoned politician from one of the larger parties challenged, "Are you suggesting that even the smallest party should have the same leadership opportunities as the major ones? We cannot subvert the will of the electorate?"

Mr. Gama nodded, "Exactly. Just as in an ecosystem, the diversity of leadership can lead to more robust and adaptive governance. This doesn't mean equal time in leadership but strategically rotating positions based on expertise and coalition needs, much like how different species take turns leading in their roles within an ecosystem. Of course, we cannot ignore the wishes of the electorate as illustrated by the proportion of respective councillors."

Mr Gama put up a slide of geese flying in V-formation and provided context. "Geese demonstrate the power of collaboration and shared leadership through their V-formation flying and rotational leadership. By flying in a V-formation, each goose benefits from the uplift created by the bird in front, significantly reducing energy expenditure and allowing them to travel further together than they could alone. They rotate the lead position, ensuring no single bird becomes overly fatigued. This strategy of mutual support and shared responsibility serves as a powerful metaphor for political parties. By working together, sharing leadership, and supporting one another, a coalition can achieve greater progress, overcome challenges, and provide better benefits and impact for all your constituents."

The room quieted, the analogy striking a chord. Discussions resumed, this time with a more cooperative tone. Parties began to see the value in sharing leadership roles, akin to how diverse species support a healthy ecosystem.

As the meeting drew to a close, agreements were reached with Mr. Gama's guidance. The coalition agreed to rotate certain leadership roles based on expertise and contribution, not just party size, and established a committee to oversee this process to ensure transparency and equity.

The first session had ended successfully, with Mr. Gama's innovative use of biomimicry principles helping to transform potential conflicts into collaborative opportunities. The councillors left the chamber not as representatives of competing parties but as members of a budding ecosystem, ready to grow together for the collective good of ABC Metro Council.

Day 2: Symbiosis and the Spirit of Shared Governance

The second day of the workshop dawned with an air of cautious optimism in the ABC Metro Council chamber. After the initial successes of the previous day, facilitated by Mr. Gama's insightful introduction to biomimicry in governance, the councillors returned, more open to unconventional approaches yet still wary of the complexities of coalition politics.

Mr. Gama greeted the assembly warmly, acknowledging the progress made. "Yesterday, we laid the foundation for a governance model inspired by nature's balance and diversity. Today, we delve deeper, exploring the concept of symbiosis—mutually beneficial relationships that sustain many of nature's most successful ecosystems."

The councillors listened intently as Mr. Gama explained symbiosis using vivid examples from nature. "Consider the relationship between clownfish and sea anemones in a coral reef. The clownfish finds shelter from predators within the anemone's tentacles, which are venomous to other fish but harmless to the clownfish due to a protective mucus layer. In return, the clownfish drives off intruders and preens the anemone, improving its health. Both parties benefit, enhancing their survival."

"This morning, we will identify potential symbiotic relationships within our council. Each party has unique strengths and resources that, if shared and leveraged collaboratively, can lead to enhanced outcomes for all," Mr. Gama proposed.

The exercise began with each party listing their primary resources, strengths, and policy focuses. The larger parties boasted significant organizational structures and funding, while the smaller parties offered grassroots connections and specialized knowledge about particular community needs.

Mr. Gama facilitated the mapping of these assets and needs, pointing out areas of potential synergy. "The Progressive Party has extensive experience in infrastructure development, and the Community Roots Party holds deep insights into local housing needs. Together, you can co-develop housing policies that are both innovative and grounded in community perspectives."

As the exercise unfolded, a sense of purpose started to replace previous tensions. Councillor Joe from a mid-sized party shared, "We have been focusing on youth programs but lack robust funding. Partnering with the National Unity Party could enhance these programs with their resources, while our grassroots engagement strategies could support their broader educational initiatives."

Encouraged by Mr. Gama, the councillors discussed how these partnerships could be formalized within the coalition agreement. It was agreed that joint committees would be established for major policy areas, co-chaired by representatives from the partnering parties. These committees would not only design but also oversee the implementation of policies, ensuring that all activities were aligned with the agreed-upon principles of mutual benefit.

To address potential conflicts and ensure transparency, Mr. Gama introduced the idea of a "Symbiosis Oversight Board"—a body that would monitor the health and productivity of these partnerships. "This board will function like the ecological regulators in nature, ensuring that the relationships remain beneficial and do not turn exploitative," he explained.

The concept of rotational leadership was revisited and refined with the symbiotic principles in mind. Leadership roles in joint committees would rotate amongst the parties, based on predefined schedules and performance reviews, ensuring that no single party could dominate the decision-making process indefinitely, whilst following the principles of equity in line with the will of the electorate.

As the session drew to a close, the councillors reflected on their discussions. The initial resistance had given way to a collaborative spirit, with each recognizing the value in the other's contribution. The agreements reached promised a balanced power structure, reflective of the council's diversity and committed to the common good.

Mr. Gama concluded, "Today, we've seen how thinking inspired by nature's symbiosis can lead us to stronger, more resilient governance structures. Let's carry this spirit forward as we continue to shape our coalition agreement."

The councillors left the chamber with a renewed sense of unity and purpose, optimistic about the possibilities of their newly forming symbiotic governance model, ready to tackle the complexities of running one of the largest cities with a collaborative and innovative approach.

Day 3: Constructing the Ecosystem - From Conflict to Collaboration

The third day of the workshop dawned bright and early, with the councillors of the ABC Metro Council gathering once again in the chamber that had, over the past two days, become a crucible for the transformation of their political relationships. Today's focus, Mr. Gama announced, would be on transforming potential conflicts into opportunities for collaboration, using principles observed in ecological conflict resolution.

"As we've seen," Mr. Gama began, "nature is not without its conflicts. However, ecosystems thrive by turning conflict into constructive interactions. Today, we will learn how to apply these principles to our coalition dynamics."

The room buzzed with a mix of intrigue and skepticism—after all, politics is often inherently adversarial. Mr. Gama smiled, understanding the underlying tensions. "Let's consider the African savannah," he suggested. "Here, predators and prey exist in a balance. This balance is crucial for the health of the savannah, allowing both to thrive without one overrunning the other."

"Similarly," he continued, "in our council, different parties are like different species in an ecosystem. Each has its role, its needs, and its contributions. Conflicts, while natural, should be managed in a way that maintains the health of our collective governance."

He proposed a scenario-based exercise: each party was to present a policy proposal they considered crucial. Other parties would then express their concerns and offer amendments, not to thwart the proposal, but to enhance its inclusivity and effectiveness.

The first proposal came from the Green Future Party, focusing on expanding public transportation to reduce the city's carbon footprint. The Industrial Growth Party expressed concerns about the potential impact on the automotive industry and job losses.

"Here lies our conflict," Mr. Gama pointed out. "Now, let's find the symbiosis." Through guided discussion, the councillors explored options such as job retraining programs, incentives for eco-friendly vehicle production, and phased implementation that could allow both environmental and industrial concerns to be addressed. The dialogue was tense but productive, with both sides beginning to see the other's perspective not as opposition but as a necessary balance.

"This," Mr. Gama noted, "is your predator-prey balance. Just as the savannah needs both the lion and the zebra, your city needs both environmental sustainability and industrial prosperity."

Encouraged by this success, the councillors moved to the next proposal—this time from the Social Harmony Party, which aimed to increase funding for cultural arts programs, arguing that it would enhance community cohesion. The Fiscal Responsibility Party resisted, citing budget constraints and more pressing needs.

Mr. Gama steered the discussion towards a creative resolution. "What if," he suggested, "we integrate these arts programs into existing community centres and schools, spreading the benefits without significant additional spending?" The parties worked together to sketch out a plan where existing facilities could be used more effectively, and local artists could be involved in education, thereby fostering community engagement without a substantial budget increase.

As the workshop progressed, Mr. Gama introduced the concept of ecological niches—each species thrives in a specific role that reduces competition for resources. For example, in a tree you find some insects on the trunk, some on the branches and others on the leaves. "Each party has its niche within the political ecosystem of our city. By defining these roles clearly in our coalition agreement, we can reduce overlaps and friction," he explained.

The day concluded with the councillors drafting a section of the coalition agreement that outlined these niches and mechanisms for conflict resolution, drawing directly from their discussions. They agreed on a structured approach to handling disputes, incorporating regular mediation sessions and an annual review to adapt the agreement to changing circumstances—a concept inspired by the adaptive strategies seen in natural ecosystems.

Mr. Gama closed the session with a reflective note: "Today, you have not only resolved specific conflicts but have also laid down a blueprint for continuous adaptation and balance. Like any thriving ecosystem, your governance model will evolve, and so will your strategies to manage conflicts."

The councillors left the chamber with a newfound respect for their diverse roles within the coalition, equipped with tools not just to coexist but to coevolve, ensuring the longevity and health of their governance ecosystem.

Day 4: Mutualistic Relationships and Governance Stability

The fourth day of the workshop opened under a canopy of hopeful anticipation among the ABC Metro Council members. Building on the foundations laid in the previous sessions, Mr. Gama prepared the councillors for the next crucial topic: establishing mutualistic relationships to ensure the stability and effectiveness of their governance.

"Today," Mr. Gama began, "we explore the principle of mutualism, where two different organisms—or in our case, political entities—work together, each benefiting from the relationship. In nature, these relationships are not just beneficial but often essential for survival. Think of this metaphorically as symbiosis and synergy on steroids."

He illustrated his point with the example of bees and flowers. "Bees collect nectar for food, and in doing so, they pollinate the flowers, enabling reproduction. Each thrives because of the other's actions. Today, let's structure our coalition agreement to foster such mutualistic relationships, ensuring that when one party succeeds, so does the coalition."

To facilitate this, Mr. Gama proposed an exercise called the Mutual Benefit Mapping. Each party was asked to outline their main goals and the resources they could offer to the coalition. The task was to identify how these goals and resources could intersect beneficially with those of other parties.

The session was structured around collaborative policy-making areas such as economic development, education, infrastructure, healthcare, and environmental sustainability. As each party presented their priorities, Mr. Gama guided them to find intersections. For instance, the Economic Growth Party was keen on enhancing local businesses, while the Social Welfare Party focused on increasing employment opportunities. These aligned through initiatives like local entrepreneurship programs that could provide both business support and create jobs.

"The essence of mutualism in our context," Mr. Gama explained, "is to create policies that are not only intersectional but also interdependent.

This way, the success of one party in achieving its goals supports another's goals, stabilizing our governance structure and distributing benefits across the board. Essentially, the whole becomes more than the sum of the parts."

The discussions were dynamic and productive, with parties beginning to appreciate the value in supporting each other's initiatives. Mr. Gama then introduced the next layer—sustainability. "Mutualistic relationships in nature are sustainable. They do not exhaust the resources of the environment they depend on. How can we ensure our policies and collaborations are sustainable?"

This question led to the integration of sustainability assessments into policy planning. The councillors agreed to establish a Sustainability Oversight Committee, tasked with reviewing all major initiatives to ensure they met environmental, economic, and social sustainability criteria before being implemented.

As the mutual benefits were mapped and discussed, Mr. Gama steered the conversation towards formalizing these relationships within the coalition agreement. "Let's define mechanisms for collaboration that include joint accountability measures," he suggested. "This way, each party is equally invested in the success of shared projects."

The councillors worked together to draft clauses in the coalition agreement that required regular joint reviews of collaborative projects, shared credit for successes, and collective strategizing for challenges. This agreement was designed to ensure that no party felt sidelined and that the successes and challenges were shared.

To close the session, Mr. Gama emphasized the importance of flexibility and adaptation. "Like any living system, a political coalition must be adaptable. It must evolve as circumstances change and learn from its experiences. Let's ensure our agreement includes provisions for periodic reviews and adjustments."

The day ended with councillors feeling more connected to each other's goals and more committed to the coalition's collective success. They recognized that by supporting one another, they were building a stronger, more resilient government.

Mr. Gama concluded, "Today, you have not only planned for mutual benefits but also built the foundations for a stable and enduring governance system. As in nature, your strength lies in your interconnectedness and your ability to adapt and support one another."

With these principles firmly embedded in their coalition agreement, the councillors left the workshop ready to enter a new era of collaborative and sustainable governance, inspired by the enduring wisdom of nature's mutualistic strategies.

Day 5: Crafting Transparency and Accountability Mechanisms

On the fifth day of the workshop, the atmosphere in the ABC Metro Council chamber was marked by a serious yet optimistic tone. Councillors were increasingly aware of the transformative journey they were undergoing. Mr. Gama, ready to address one of the most crucial aspects of governance, opened the day with a clear focus: "Today, we tackle transparency and accountability. These are the pillars that will uphold the trust between you and the electorate, as well as among yourselves within the coalition."

Drawing again from nature, Mr. Gama began with an analogy. "Consider the role of sunlight in an ecosystem—it enables growth, sustains life, and provides energy. Transparency in governance plays a similar role, illuminating actions, ensuring they are visible and understandable to all."

To bring this concept into practical terms, Mr. Gama introduced the first task of the day: designing a Transparency Charter for the coalition. This charter would outline how decisions are made, disclose who is involved in the decision-making processes, and specify how information is shared both internally and with the public.

The councillors were divided into groups, each tasked with drafting sections of the charter. Key elements discussed included the publication of meeting agendas and minutes, the declaration of conflicts of interest, and mechanisms for public feedback on legislative proposals.

Mr. Gama then shifted the focus to accountability. "Transparency is the light, and accountability is what grows under that light. It involves not only adhering to rules and regulations but also actively demonstrating responsibility for your actions to those you serve."

To institutionalize accountability, Mr. Gama proposed the creation of an Independent Oversight Committee (IOC). This body would be empowered to audit coalition activities, review compliance with the coalition agreement, and investigate any allegations of misconduct. Importantly, it would include members from outside the political sphere—experts in law, ethics, and community development—to ensure impartiality.

The councillors engaged deeply with this proposal, discussing the composition of the IOC, the scope of its authority, and the process for handling its findings. They agreed that the IOC should report not only to the council but also directly to the public, ensuring an additional layer of transparency.

As part of this discussion, Mr. Gama introduced a feedback loop mechanism inspired by ecological systems. "In nature, feedback loops help maintain balance. Negative feedback reduces the intensity of changes, while positive feedback amplifies them. For example, the predator-prey dynamics between lions and zebras illustrate a **negative feedback loop**, where predation by lions reduces the zebra population, which in turn controls the lion population, maintaining balance in the ecosystem. Conversely, the interaction between elephant grazing and tree density illustrates a **positive feedback loop**, where elephant behaviour leads to reduced tree density, promoting grassland expansion and increasing the populations of grazing herbivores, further amplifying the initial change. Similarly, in governance, feedback from the public can help you adjust your policies and actions effectively."

Councillors worked together to outline how these feedback loops would function. They planned regular public forums and digital platforms where citizens could express their concerns and make suggestions, including on development priorities. The feedback collected through these channels would be reviewed quarterly by the council, and necessary adjustments to policies and practices would be made accordingly.

The final task of the day was integrating these mechanisms into the coalition agreement. Each group presented their sections of the Transparency Charter and the operational guidelines for the IOC. These presentations were followed by a rigorous debate and revision session, ensuring every clause was clear, actionable, and agreed upon by all.

Mr. Gama concluded the session with a reflective note: "By committing to transparency and establishing robust accountability mechanisms, you are not just promising to serve the public but also equipping yourselves with the tools to fulfil that promise effectively. You are building trust, and with trust, the resilience of your coalition will grow."

As the councillors left the chamber, there was a palpable sense of accomplishment and responsibility. They had laid down a comprehensive framework that would not only guide their coalition but also strengthen the fabric of their governance through transparency and accountability. This framework promised a new era of open and responsible government for ABC Metro Council, inspired by the self-regulating, transparent, and accountable systems found in nature.

Day 6: Fostering Resilience and Adaptability in Governance

The sixth day of the workshop marked the culmination of a transformative week for the ABC Metro Council. As the councillors settled into their seats, a sense of determination and anticipation filled the room. Today, Mr. Gama would guide them through the final principles necessary for a robust coalition: resilience and adaptability.

"Good morning, everyone," Mr. Gama started, his voice reflecting the gravity and excitement of the semi-final day. "Over the past days, we've laid down a foundation based on mutualism, transparency, and accountability. Today, we focus on ensuring our governance structure is not only strong but also flexible and responsive to change. This is about building resilience and adaptability into the very core of our coalition."

Mr. Gama introduced the day's first concept: ecological resilience, the ability of an ecosystem to absorb disturbances and still retain its basic function and structure. "In governance, this translates to your coalition's ability to handle crises and unforeseen changes without falling apart," he explained.

To illustrate, Mr. Gama used the example of a forest ecosystem that can regenerate after a fire. "Just as the forest regrows, often more diverse and robust than before, your governance should be able to learn and evolve from challenges."

The first exercise of the day involved scenario planning. Councillors were asked to envision potential crises that could impact their governance—economic downturns, public health emergencies such as pandemics, or political scandals—and then brainstorm procedural responses that could be encoded into the coalition agreement to manage these effectively.

"Let's think about a scenario where there's a sudden economic downturn," Mr. Gama suggested. "What mechanisms within our coalition agreement can ensure that the most vulnerable communities do not bear the brunt of this crisis? How can we adjust our budget allocations swiftly and ethically?"

Councillors discussed various mechanisms, such as a crisis response fund and flexible budget clauses that could be activated based on predefined economic indicators. They also considered the importance of maintaining open lines of communication with the public during crises, ensuring transparency in how decisions are made under pressure.

Next, Mr. Gama shifted the focus to adaptability in governance. "Adaptability is about more than just surviving crises," he stated. "It's about thriving in a changing environment, learning from experiences, and continuously improving."

To foster this adaptability, Mr. Gama introduced the idea of a 'Living Document' approach to the coalition agreement. Unlike static documents, a Living Document is regularly reviewed and updated to reflect new insights, changes in the political landscape, and the evolving needs of the community.

Councillors were guided to draft a process for regular review of the coalition agreement, including annual evaluation meetings with independent facilitators who could help assess the coalition's performance against its goals and suggest amendments based on outcomes and feedback.

The final discussion of the day—and of the workshop—cantered on embedding a culture of continuous learning within the council. Mr. Gama encouraged the establishment of a Governance Innovation Lab, a dedicated team within the council that would regularly experiment with new governance models on a small scale, evaluate their effectiveness, and recommend wider implementation if successful.

As the workshop drew to a close, Mr. Gama commended the councillors for their dedication and visionary approach. "You have not only committed to working together but have also embraced principles that prepare your coalition for the future, whatever it may hold."

The councillors, inspired by the week's work, expressed their appreciation for the workshop's insights. They recognized that the principles embedded in their new coalition agreement would guide them in not just governing effectively but in leading ABC Metro Council with a commitment to resilience, adaptability, and continuous improvement.

Leaving the chamber, the councillors felt equipped to face the complexities of governing a diverse and dynamic city. The new coalition agreement, enriched with ecological wisdom and practical strategies for sustainable governance, promised a future where ABC Metro Council could thrive, adaptable and resilient, whatever challenges it might face.

Day 7: Integration and Implementation of Coalition Principles

On the seventh and final day of the workshop, the ABC Metro Council members gathered with a sense of accomplishment and anticipation. Over the past week, under Mr. Gama's guidance, they had traversed the complex terrain of coalition politics, learning to draw from the principles of biomimicry to craft a resilient and adaptable governance framework. Today's session was dedicated to integrating these principles into a cohesive coalition agreement and planning for its effective implementation.

Mr. Gama opened the day with words of encouragement and focus. "Today, we bring together all that we have learned and agreed upon. We will integrate these insights into a unified document that will guide your governance. More importantly, we will devise a clear plan for the implementation of this agreement, ensuring that the spirit and letter of what we have crafted does not get lost in translation to day-to-day governance."

The morning session began with a comprehensive review of the draft coalition agreement. The document was projected on a large screen, each clause and section open for final adjustments. Mr. Gama facilitated this review meticulously, ensuring that the language used was clear, the responsibilities defined were equitable, and the mechanisms for transparency and adaptability were practical.

"Let's go through this document together, ensuring that each part not only reflects our discussions but is also actionable and measurable," Mr. Gama directed. As they progressed, councillors were invited to voice any concerns or suggest last-minute adjustments. This process was crucial to ensure full buy-in from all parties, as the agreement needed unanimous approval to be adopted.

Following the document review, the focus shifted to the implementation plan. Mr. Gama introduced a phased approach to implementation, emphasizing the need for gradual integration of the new practices to allow sufficient time for adjustments and training.

"Phase one will involve immediate actions, such as the establishment of the Independent Oversight Committee and the Transparency Charter. Phase two will focus on the integration of more complex systems like the Sustainability Oversight Committee and the Governance Innovation Lab," explained Mr. Gama.

He further highlighted the importance of training and capacity building for all council members and their staff. "Everyone involved in governance must understand not only what changes are being made but also why they are important and how they can be a part of these changes. We will organize a series of workshops and training sessions over the next three months."

To facilitate the transition, Mr. Gama proposed the creation of a Transition Team, composed of representatives from each party and chaired by a neutral expert in public administration. This team would oversee the implementation process, address any issues that arise, and maintain the momentum of change.

The afternoon was dedicated to detailing this Transition Team's structure, roles, and responsibilities. Councillors discussed and debated the best practices for managing change, drawing from their own experiences and the knowledge they had gained during the workshop.

As the final hour of the workshop approached, Mr. Gama invited each councillor to reflect on the week's journey and share their thoughts. Many expressed a renewed sense of purpose and optimism about the coalition's future, highlighting how the workshop had transformed their approach to governance and collaboration.

In his closing remarks, Mr. Gama congratulated the councillors on their commitment and hard work. "You have set a new standard for what collaborative governance can look like. The principles of biomimicry— adaptability, resilience, mutual benefit—these are now embedded in your coalition agreement, ready to guide you in governing this vibrant city."

The workshop concluded with the formal signing of the coalition agreement, each party leader affirming their commitment to the principles and processes laid out in the document. Applause filled the room as they each signed, marking the beginning of a new chapter for the ABC Metro Council.

As councillors left the chamber, they carried with them not just a document but a new vision for governance, inspired by nature and refined through collaboration and mutual respect. The days ahead would be filled with challenges, no doubt, but the foundations laid during this transformative week promised a future of innovative, inclusive, and effective governance for ABC Metro Council.

Abridged Coalition Agreement for The ABC Metro Council

Preamble

This Coalition Agreement is established by the undersigned parties of the ABC Metro Council, recognizing the necessity of collaborative governance following the election results which did not allow any single party to assume an absolute majority. Inspired by principles of biomimicry that emphasize sustainability, resilience, adaptability, and mutual benefits, this agreement aims to ensure effective, transparent, and inclusive governance for the betterment of our community.

Article 1: Purpose and Principles

1. **Purpose**: The purpose of this agreement is to establish a stable and effective coalition government that represents and serves the diverse interests of the ABC Metro Council community, ensuring prosperity and fairness.

2. **Principles**:

   - **Mutual Respect**: Each party acknowledges the value and contributions of other coalition members.

   - **Transparency**: All actions taken under this coalition will be transparent with active communication to the public.

   - **Accountability**: Parties agree to uphold the highest standards of integrity and accountability.

- **Adaptability**: The coalition commits to remaining adaptable to changing circumstances and responsive to public needs.

- **Equity**: Decision-making and leadership roles will be distributed equitably among coalition parties.

- **Existence**: The coalition exists and collapses as a collective and serves at the pleasure of the electorate.

Article 2: Governance Structure

1. **Coalition Council**: A Coalition Council comprising representatives from each party will oversee the coalition's activities.

2. **Leadership Rotation**: Leadership roles within key committees will rotate among coalition parties, based on expertise and equitable representation.

3. **Independent Oversight Committee (IOC)**: An IOC will be established to monitor the coalition's adherence to this agreement and investigate any allegations of misconduct. The IOC it will include members from outside the political sphere—experts in law, ethics, and community development.

Article 3: Decision-Making Process

1. **Consensus Building**: Decisions affecting the coalition's policies will strive for consensus among all parties. In situations where consensus cannot be achieved, a supermajority of 75% will be required.

2. **Emergency Decisions**: In urgent situations demanding immediate action, the Coalition Council can make decisions with a temporary simple majority, pending a full review within 30 days.

Article 4: Transparency and Accountability

1. **Transparency Charter**: A Transparency Charter will be implemented detailing all processes, meetings, and decisions, which will be accessible to the public.

2. **Public Engagement**: Regular public forums and digital platforms will be established for citizens to express concerns, offer suggestions, and provide feedback on governance.

Article 5: Adaptability and Review

1. **Regular Reviews**: The coalition agreement will be reviewed annually, with provisions for amendments to adapt to new challenges and opportunities.

2. **Governance Innovation Lab**: An innovation lab will be created to explore and test new governance models and strategies, enhancing the coalition's adaptability.

Article 6: Conflict Resolution

1. **Mediation and Arbitration**: A formal process for mediation and arbitration will be established to address and resolve conflicts within the coalition promptly and fairly.

Article 7: Implementation and Monitoring

1. **Transition Team**: A Transition Team will oversee the implementation of this agreement and the initial setup of the coalition's governance structures.

2. **Performance Metrics**: Specific performance metrics will be established to evaluate the effectiveness of the coalition governance, with periodic and annual reports made public.

Article 8: Duration and Termination

1. **Duration**: This agreement is effective immediately upon signing and will remain in effect until the next municipal elections unless reviewed, amended, or terminated by consensus of the coalition parties.

2. **Termination**: Should the coalition agreement be deemed unworkable or terminated by the electorate through a process managed by the **Independent Oversight Committee (IOC)** fresh elections will be conducted within a reasonable time.

Signatures

This agreement is signed this ___ day of ___________, 20XX, by the following parties, each represented by their duly authorized representatives:

- [Party 1], Signature:

- [Party 2], Signature:

- [Party 3], Signature:

- [Party 4], Signature:

- [Party 5], Signature:

- [Party 6], Signature:

By signing this agreement, each party commits to the principles and processes outlined herein, dedicating themselves to collaborative and effective governance for the ABC Metro Municipality.

About the Author

Gamelihle Sibanda may not be a politician, but his vast reservoir of multidisciplinary knowledge offers him a unique bird's-eye view on a myriad of subjects. Dive into this book where he dons the fascinating lens of biomimicry (innovation inspired by nature) – drawing inspiration directly from the marvels of nature – to shed light on coalitions and how strategies from nature can make them more stable. Remember, we humans are woven into the intricate tapestry of nature. By embracing the wisdom of the ecosystems we inhabit and aligning with the harmonious dance of species around us, we stand to gain immeasurable insights. Dive in and discover nature's playbook for thriving coalitions!

Disclaimer!

If you do not agree with the ideas in this book, please do not shoot the messenger, share your alternative viable ideas so others can learn from you.

www.ingramcontent.com/pod-product-compliance
Lightning Source LLC
Chambersburg PA
CBHW051841250726
48659CB00005B/1963